Published by Scholastic Inc., *Publishers since 1920.* SCHOLASTIC and associated logos are trademarks and/or registered trademarks of Scholastic Inc.

The publisher does not have any control over and does not assume any responsibility for author or third-party websites or their content.

This book is a work of fiction. Names, characters, places, and incidents are either the product of the author's imagination or are used fictitiously, and any resemblance to actual persons, living or dead, business establishments, events, or locales is entirely coincidental.

ISBN 978-0-545-90881-8

10 9 8 7 6 5 4 3 2 1   15 16 17 18 19

Printed in the U.S.A.   40
First printing 2015
Text by Howie Dewin
Book design by Two Red Shoes Design

Every generation needs a voice.
So you want to find yours, huh?
We totally get it.

"Finding your voice" is the same thing as finding yourself. It's your point of view, your ideas, your opinions.

It can take a little while to know all that stuff about yourself, but it's worth the work. Because knowing who you are means knowing what you want to say—and how you want to say it.

We each took a section of this book to share some of the stuff we've figured out about ourselves. Not just the public stuff we all share online, but also our secret selves—the stuff we don't talk about much. That's the stuff that helps you really figure out who you are.

So go on, take a look. Maybe it'll help you figure out a little bit more about yourself. Maybe it'll help *you* find *your* voice!

Love,

Jerrica, Kimber, Aja & Shana

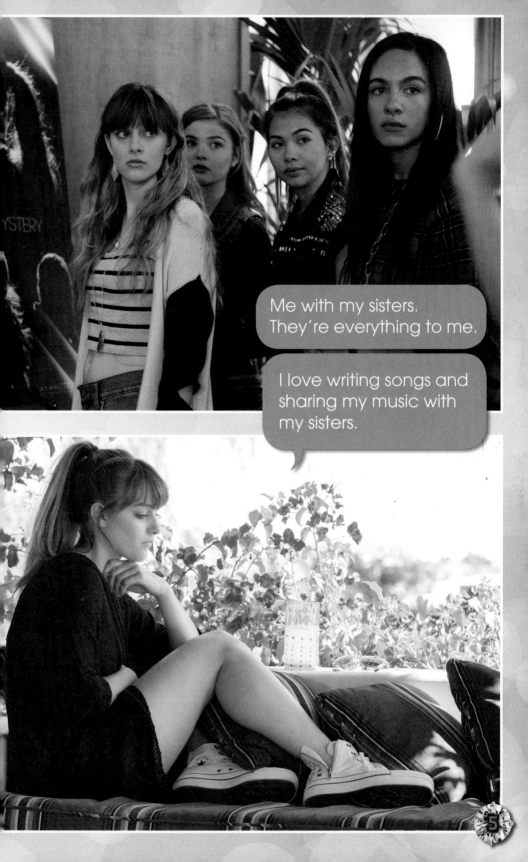

He used to call me his diamond in the rough. His "Jem."

And this is Aunt Bailey, the best foster mom in the world.

Aunt Bailey always believes in my sisters and me.

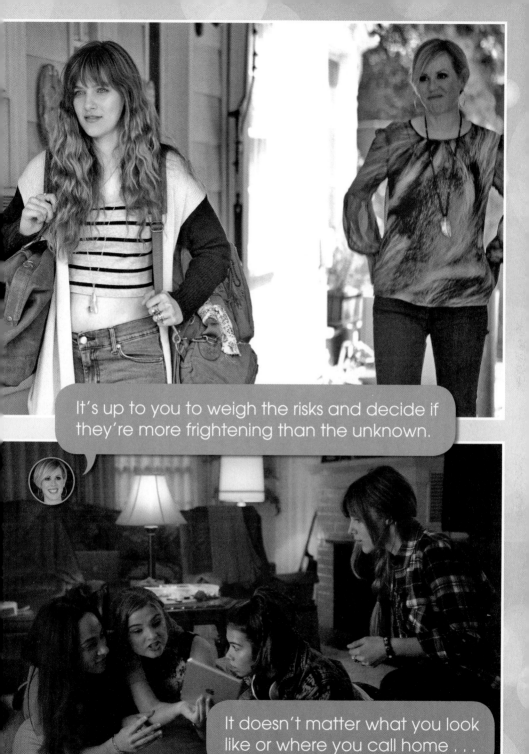

. . . when my sisters and I are together, nothing else matters.

This is Synergy, one of my dad's best creations.

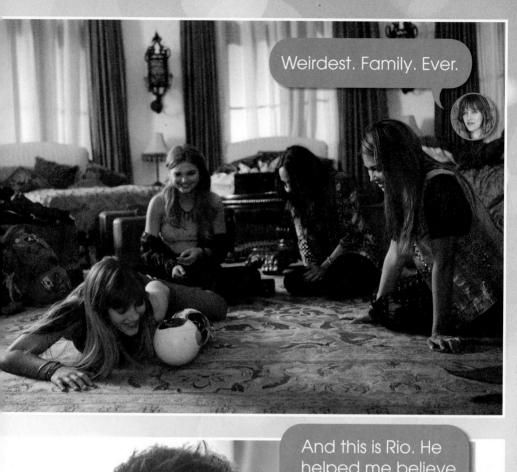

Weirdest. Family. Ever.

And this is Rio. He helped me believe in my voice. A lot more on him later!

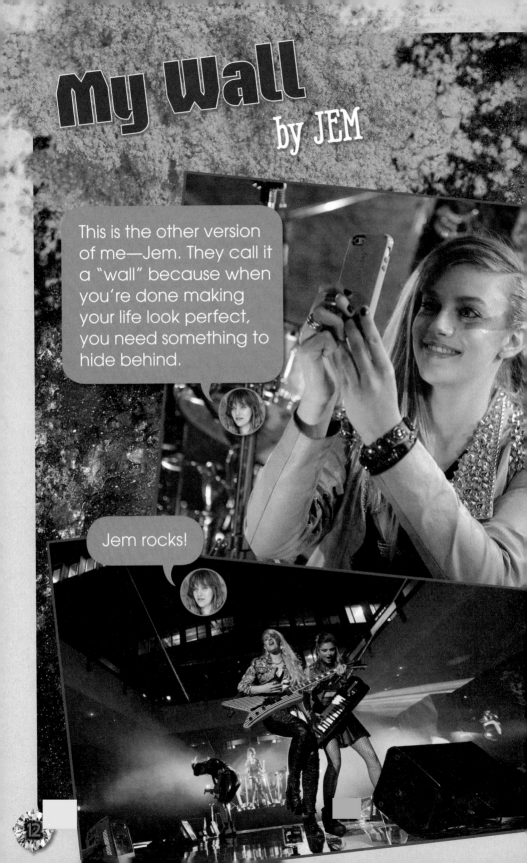

My Wall
by JEM

This is the other version of me—Jem. They call it a "wall" because when you're done making your life look perfect, you need something to hide behind.

Jem rocks!

And she's definitely not the same person as Jerrica.

Balancing fame and family can be tricky. The key is to remember who you really are.

Find Your Voice!

Aunt Bailey always told me some voices are too special to keep hidden. Are you ready to share *your* voice? Answer these questions to uncover the real you.

1 What activity gets you so excited and engrossed that you lose all track of time? _____ _____

2 When you need to relax, you . . . _____ _____ _____

3 What do you do when you need to cheer up? _____ _____ _____

4 What books (or kinds of book) make you forget how many pages you've read? _____ _____

5 What's your favorite kind of movie? Do you prefer movies that make you laugh or ones that make you cry? _____ _____

6 How would you describe the person who understands you the best? _____
_____

7 What kind of advice do your friends ask you for? _____
_____
_____

8 What would your friends say if they were trying to sound like you? _____
_____

9 What always makes you laugh? Feel sad? Get angry? _____
_____
_____

10 What kind of music makes you smile? _____
_____

The better you know what makes you feel happy, sad, or excited, the closer you are to finding your voice.

Are you like me?

Do you know your own voice?
Answer these questions to find out!

1. When someone asks you to do something, what's the first thing you think?
   A. *I wonder what everyone else will do?*
   B. *I'm not sure if I should or not.*
   C. *Absolutely YES* (or) *Absolutely NO!*

2. When your teacher calls on you in class and you don't know the answer, you . . .
   A. announce, "I don't know, but I'd like to know."
   B. stare blankly and sink down in your seat.
   C. ask if you can be excused to go to the bathroom.

3. When you go to a movie with a friend, what do you say to her afterward?

A. "It was okay."

B. "I really loved _____" (or) "I really didn't like _____."

C. "What did you think?"

• • • • • • • • • •

4. You are given a writing assignment at school. What happens when the teacher tells you to start writing?

A. You think about all the things the teacher said you had to include. You struggle with every word, but end up getting all the requirements into your story.

B. You stare at the blank paper. Next thing you know, you're waking up from a nap.

C. You write the idea you've been thinking about for two days, and then add the elements your teacher said you had to include.

• • • • • • • • • •

5. When you get into a disagreement with someone, what do you say to yourself when it's over?

A. "I wish I'd said _____! Why don't I ever think of a smart comeback in the moment?"

B. "I wish I had just kept my mouth shut."

C. "I am glad I said what I did. I hope we can move past this."

• • • • • • • • • •

6. You're out with a group, and don't like the plan everyone else is into. So you . . .

A. sneak away and go home.

B. go along with whatever the group is going to do—who knows, it could turn out to be fun!

C. interrupt the conversation and state your point of view.

Turn to page 60 for your Jem personality analysis.

My Wall
by KIMBER BENTON

This is me, Kimber. There's only one version of me—and that version *loves* it when there's a camera around!

Internet famous. The next best thing to being ACTUALLY famous!

A few of my favorite words: *Hair and makeup!*

Jerrica and I are opposites—except for one thing: Family comes first.

Whatever it is you're scared of, you don't have to be.

Just be yourself—and sing what you feel!

My favorite color: sparkle!
My Go Bag
My fabulous boots!
Me bein' *sooo* LA!
My bling convention!

My Top Ten Ways to Become a YouTube Sensation

1 Decide what you want to do.

2 Practice that thing until you are as good as you can possibly be.

3 Do that thing in front of a camera.

4 Do that thing in front of a camera about a hundred more times! Don't stop till you record the best possible version of it.

5 Show your friends and family what you've done and get their approval and support. (These people will be your biggest fans—and the ones who will share the link to your video before anyone else. Plus they'll probably do it lots of times!)

6 Upload your video.

7 DON'T sit and stare at the number of hits.

8 DO send out alerts to your friends and family.

9 Take a little break and hang with your sisters.

10 Go back to #1 and do it all over again.

Are you like me?

Would you like life in the spotlight?
Take this quiz to find out!

1. When you go to a party, you . . .
   A. find the host and ask if he or she needs help.
   B. search for your friends and spend the whole party with them.
   C. spend most of the party talking to people you've just met.

   • • • • • • • • • •

2. When you see a performer you really like, you . . .
   A. really wish you could meet her or him.
   B. really wish you were her or him.
   C. really wish you could have your chance on stage.

3. When someone pulls out a camera, you . . .
   A. jump into the middle of the frame.
   B. cover your face and turn away.
   C. quietly strike a pose on the off-chance you end up in the picture.

• • • • • • • • •

4. When someone gives you a compliment, you . . .
   A. laugh and say something silly about yourself.
   B. compliment the person who complimented you.
   C. smile, say thank you, and continue whatever you were doing.

• • • • • • • • •

5. When you are somewhere with a dance floor, you . . .
   A. sit back and enjoy watching everyone get down.
   B. jump into the group and have a great time.
   C. boogie down just crazy enough that you clear your own area on the dance floor.

• • • • • • • • •

6. When you have downtime, you . . .
   A. get busy on an art project.
   B. have a movie marathon.
   C. call friends and figure out a time to get together.

Check out page 61 for your custom Kimber personality analysis!

My Wall

by AJA LEITH

I let my bumper stickers do the talking!

PART-TIME GENIUS!

FULL-TIME REBEL!

It's all about how you're wired!

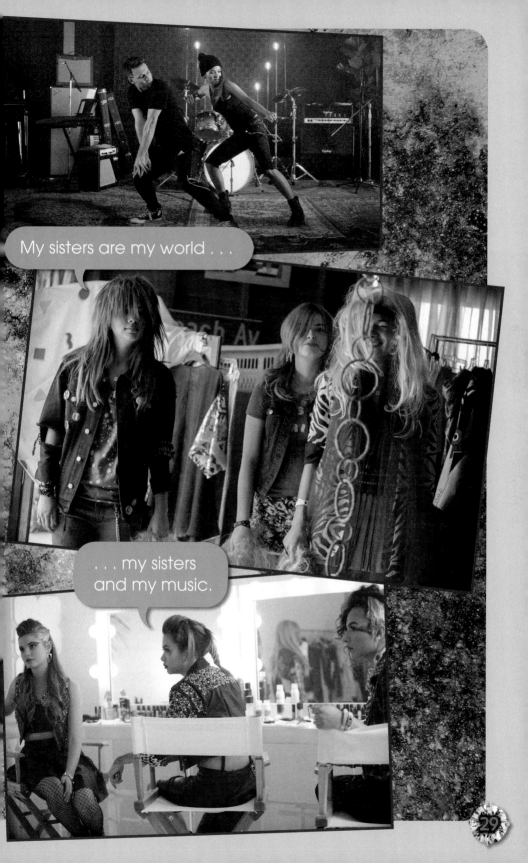

My sisters are my world . . .

. . . my sisters and my music.

My Top Ten Ways to Be Totally Cutting-Edge Cool

1 Read blogs, newspapers, magazines . . . anything that keeps you informed.

2 Talk to people about what THEY are doing.

3 LISTEN when people talk to you.

4 Always keep your eyes open and your head up (as in, don't spend all your time looking at your phone!).

5 If something catches your eye and you think it's cool, find out more about it.

6 Keep an open mind about WHAT you think is cool.

7 Keep an open mind about WHO you think is cool.

8 Don't confuse being mean with being cutting-edge cool. It's never cool to act mean.

9 Don't be afraid to be UNcool!

10 Before you do anything about anything, ask yourself these questions: Do I really like this thing? Do I really want to do this thing? Check in with that little voice inside you that always tells you the truth. That's your **voice**, by the way!

Are you like me?

Do you live to test the limits and the rules? Take this quiz to find out!

1. When someone tells you how to do something, your reaction is . . .
   A. "Thanks for that information."
   B. "Thanks, but if I wanted your advice, I'd ask for it."
   C. "Okay, but why don't we try it my way?"

   • • • • • • • • • • •

2. If something looks a little dangerous, you . . .
   A. turn and go far, far away.
   B. jump right in! It looks exciting.
   C. wait to see what everybody else is doing.

3. What are you most likely to get in trouble for?
   A. Not being on time
   B. Not picking up your room
   C. Doing something you've been told you're not supposed to do

4. When you do something you're not sure you should be doing, you feel . . .
   A. sick
   B. scared
   C. thrilled

5. How often do you get called a daredevil?
   A. All the time
   B. Sometimes
   C. Never

6. When you play a new game or put together a new gadget, what do you do with the directions?
   A. Read them first, and then proceed.
   B. Look at them occasionally, but don't worry if what you're doing doesn't match the directions.
   C. What directions?

Check out page 62 for your Aja personality analysis.

My Wall
by SHANA ELMSFORD

Make the most of what you've got . . . that's my motto!

Drumsticks—the ultimate fashion accessory.

And the pushing . . .

Plus everyone's always asking for your advice!

My Top Ten Ways to Find Your Fashion Sense

1 Before throwing anything away, ask yourself this question: Can I turn this into something totally stylish? [Such as, "Could this old flowered bedsheet become a maxi dress?"] Hint: The answer is almost always YES!

2 Figure out the answer to this question: What season are you? Spring (light, pastel colors)? Summer (bright colors)? Fall (greens, browns)? Or winter (white, pale blue)?

3 Every time you see a piece of clothing you like, take a picture.

4 Review your fashion photo collection and make a list of things you notice often—like specific colors, styles, fabrics, or combinations.

5 Keep a log with a photo of you in every outfit you wore that week. List each day's high points and low points. At the end of the week, look back over each picture and assess your fashion feats and fiascos.

6 Picture your perfect day. What are you wearing?

7 Try on clothes that you don't necessarily like when they're hanging on a hanger. They might surprise you.

8 Listen to other people's opinions. Then make your own decisions.

9 Don't be afraid to "borrow" ideas from other people.

10 Once you find the fashion you like, don't be afraid to wear it!

Are you like me?

Take this quiz to find out.

1. Do you notice what someone's wearing before you notice the expression on her/his face?
   A. Yes
   B. No
   C. Sometimes

2. Do you know the difference between clothing and accessories?
   A. Yes
   B. No
   C. Who cares?

3. When you pick up a magazine, do you look at ads instead
   of articles?
   A. Yes
   B. No
   C. Only if I'm interested in the product.

   • • • • • • • • • •

4. Do people comment on your style?
   A. Yes, all the time
   B. No, almost never
   C. Sometimes

   • • • • • • • • • •

5. Do you care what people say about your style?
   A. Yes
   B. No
   C. Only if it's negative.

   • • • • • • • • • •

6. If you were told you had to shop for seven days straight,
   would that be a good thing or a bad thing?
   A. It would be a GREAT thing.
   B. It would be awful!
   C. It'd be good—but only if it were with someone else's money.

Check out page 63 for your Shana personality analysis.

41

This is home . . .

Greetings from Pineview, California!

There's no place like home . . .
Or as Kimber would say . . .

There's no place like home page!

The ultimate front-porch rocker!

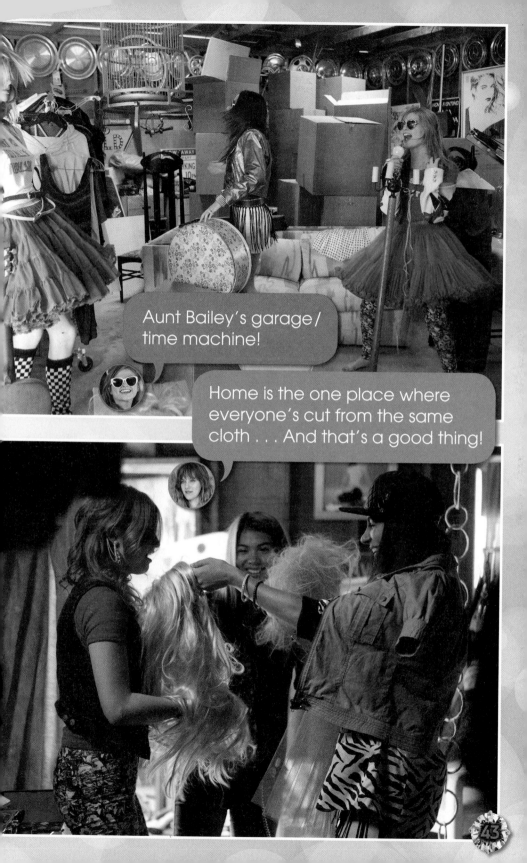

Aunt Bailey's garage/time machine!

Home is the one place where everyone's cut from the same cloth . . . And that's a good thing!

...and this is
life in LA.

Let's be honest . . . at some point, we've all wanted to become someone else.

You're telling me?

Talk about love at first sight!

Welcome to Starlight Enterprises

STARLIGHT
ENTERPRISES

ERICA RAYMOND, CEO

Ladies and Gentleman . . . Erica Raymond, Founder and CEO of Starlight Enterprises

My job is to see that every act reaches its full potential. That means changing they way they act, the way they sound . . . and the way they look.

You're giving us new looks?

I already have!

Orange hair.
Orange makeup.
Orange everything!

Good for hiding all
your old handbags

Tough and
feminine at
the same time

A.E. [After Erica]

Tries just
hard enough

Just the right
amount of bling

Ripped ... but in
a good way

A.E. [After Erica]

53

Not trying at all!

Did these come out of the "pioneer clothing" trunk?

Are you sure that's not upside down?

B.E. [Before Erica]

Interesting . . .

Last season . . .
thirty years ago

Nice . . . back when
they were in style

B.E. [Before Erica]

Stylish

Designer

Trendy

A.E. [After Erica]

Sometimes all people need is a chance to surprise you.

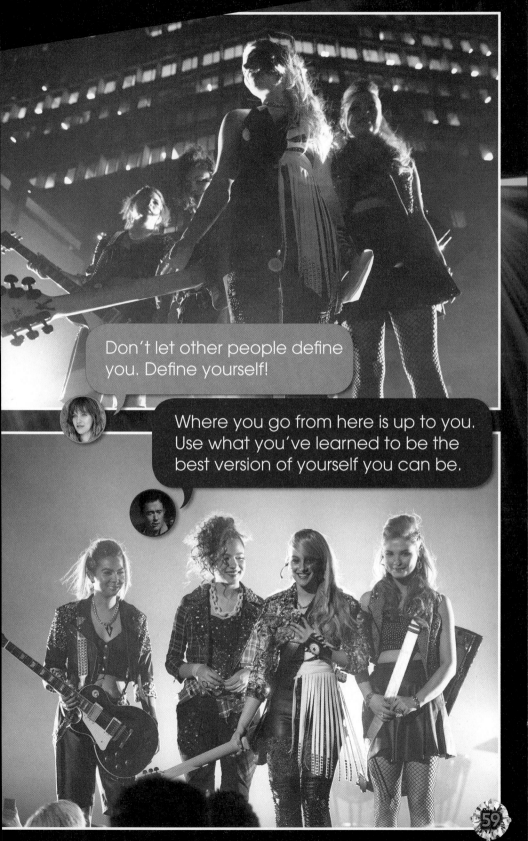

Don't let other people define you. Define yourself!

Where you go from here is up to you. Use what you've learned to be the best version of yourself you can be.

JEM Personality Analysis

So do you think you know your own voice? Let's check it out! Score your answers with the points below.

1) a=1, b=2, c=3   2) a=3, b=1, c=2
3) a=1, b=3, c=2   4) a=2, b=1, c=3
5) a=2, b=1, c=3   6) a=2, b=1, c=3

6 to 9
KEEP LISTENING!

Finding your voice and really knowing what you think is a long process. Everyone finds their voice in their own way and in their own time. Just keep asking yourself questions, and then listen carefully to what that little voice inside you says in response!

10 to 13
YOU'RE ON THE RIGHT TRACK!

You understand and speak your true feelings about things, but you don't always take the time to ask yourself the tough questions. Or maybe you don't always want to follow your own advice! Either way, congratulations on finding your voice—just make sure you use it!

14 to 18
YOU KNOW YOUR VOICE!

You know your voice, and you use it! Congratulations! Now the challenge is to make sure you use your voice to help others and make things better in the world. (And make sure you don't use it so loudly that you drown out others!)

KIMBER Personality Analysis

Are you cut out for life in the spotlight? Score your answers with the points below.

1) a=1, b=2, c=3
2) a=1, b=2, c=3
3) a=3, b=1, c=2
4) a=1, b=2, c=3
5) a=1, b=2, c=3
6) a=2, b=1, c=3

6 to 9
YOU ARE A WONDERFUL AUDIENCE!

You would be a great best friend for Kimber . . . because you are a wonderful audience member. You are supportive and really enjoy other people who enjoy the spotlight—but the spotlight is not the place for you! The world is a better place because of people like you.

10 to 13
LIKE, NOT LOVE . . .

You don't necessarily go searching for the spotlight, but if it happens to land on you, you won't run away. And it just might turn out that you deserve it . . . so don't be shy!

14 to 18
YOU LIVE FOR THE SPOTLIGHT!

You always find a light, even on a pitch-black night! You were born to be in the spotlight. You like the way it feels, and others like watching you there. Just remember, occasionally others deserve a moment there, too!

AJA Personality Analysis

Are you a rebel like Aja? Score your answers with the points below.

1) a=1, b=2, c=3   2) a=1, b=3, c=2
3) a=2, b=1, c=3   4) a=1, b=2, c=3
5) a=3, b=2, c=1   6) a=1, b=2, c=3

6 to 9
SMART AND PRACTICAL

You would be a very good friend for Aja because you'd help balance out her rule-breaking ways. Thanks to you and people like you, there is order in the world——and lots of situations are way better (and safer!) than they would be otherwise.

10 to 13
CURIOUS BUT SAFE

You are a great combination of practical and curious. You aren't afraid of trying new things, but you don't do anything without thinking it through. You should never be afraid of expressing your opinion to others because your ability to weigh the pros and cons is extremely valuable!

14 to 18
FULL-TIME REBEL!

Life is always exciting with you in the mix. You will try things that could lead to wonderful new discoveries. But you must be careful! Your "jump in with both feet" attitude can lead to trouble——not just for you, but for the people around you. Learn how to think things through without losing your spirit!

SHANA Personality Analysis

Are you a fashion trendsetter? Score your answers with the points below.

1) a=3, b=1, c=2   2) a=3, b=2, c=1
3) a=3, b=1, c=2   4) a=3, b=1, c=2
5) a=3, b=1, c=2   6) a=3, b=1, c=2

6 to 9
JUST WEAR A UNIFORM!

You have other things on your mind besides fashion. You would probably be just as happy to wear the same thing every day—and the simpler the better. Lots of very smart and successful people are like you. They don't want to use their brainpower on style—they save that energy for their work. So wear your "uniform" with pride!

10 to 13
YOU LOOK SWELL!

You like to look good, and you feel better when feel like you look good. But it's not the most important thing in your life. You also know that how you look is not totally wrapped up in what you're wearing. A lot of what makes a person "look good" has to do with who they are on the inside.

14 to 18
SASSY AND STYLIN'!

You are the go-to person for what's new and hot. You also know how to make an amazing outfit out of a pile of rags. There is a lot of creativity and passion in your love of clothes and style, and that's great. Because happy, successful people are pretty much always overflowing with creativity and passion!